TASTE OF THE
CARIBBEAN

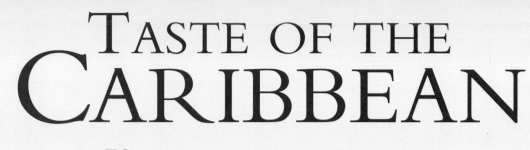

Taste of the Caribbean

70 simple-to-cook recipes

Rosamund Grant

SMITHMARK

This edition published in 1995
by SMITHMARK Publishers Inc.
16 East 32nd Street
New York
NY 10016
USA

SMITHMARK books are available for bulk purchase for sales and
promotion and premium use. For details write or call the manager of
special sales.
SMITHMARK Publishers Inc.
16 East 32nd Street
New York
NY 10016
(212) 532–6600

ISBN 0–8317–7892–X

Publisher: Joanna Lorenz
Senior Cookery Editor: Linda Fraser
Cookery Editor: Anne Hildyard
Copy Editor: Christine Ingram
Designer: Siân Keogh
Photography and styling: Patrick McLeavey, assisted by Rebecca Sturrock
Food for Photography: Joanne Craig assisted by Curtis Edwards
Illustrator: Madeleine David

Printed in Singapore by Star Standard Industries Pte. Ltd.

ACKNOWLEDGEMENTS
The author wishes to thank Chandis for all her hard work typing the
manuscript, Gale for help with the Barbadian Coconut Sweet Bread, and her
children Joanna, Nayo and Chris, for all their practical help.

Pictures on page 1 and top right page 7: Zefa Pictures Ltd
Pictures on pages 2, 3, and bottom left page 7: Greg Evans International Photo Library

CONTENTS

INTRODUCTION

A *Taste of the Caribbean* features recipes that reflect the rich diversity of traditions and culture that is the hallmark of the Caribbean. People of many different races and cultures have lived in the Caribbean islands over the centuries and their presence changed not only the history of the islands, but also profoundly influenced its cuisine. With each set of people came their traditional cooking methods, they imported their own favorite foods, planting fruit and vegetables and rearing livestock. Gradually over the years the various islanders embraced these traditions as their own and today we have to realise that what we think of as Caribbean cooking, is actually a blend of food and cooking traditions from all over the world.

The first inhabitants of the Caribbean were the Arawak Indians who sailed from the Americas. They surely must have thought they had found paradise in these islands, with fresh fish from the seas, and yams, sweet potatoes, papayas, pineapples and guavas growing in abundance.

Jerked pork, a traditional Caribbean dish, where the whole pig is spit roasted over a slow fire, is almost certainly of Arawak tradition. The Arawaks were skilled hunters and fishermen, they cultivated crops, chiefly cassava, from which they derived a variety of products and they were renowned for their intricately designed and attractively patterned arts and crafts.

The Europeans, who colonised the region in the early sixteenth century, also had a significant influence. They experimented with the cultivation of bananas, plantains, coconut, sugar cane, oranges, limes and ginger – crops that then were new to the island, and today we think of as essentially Caribbean. Along with sugar cane, cotton and coffee began to be grown on plantations for the export trade.

The tropical islands of the Caribbean stretch from the coast of South America out into the Atlantic ocean.

Cod, which had been salted and stored in the ship's hold on its long journey from Europe to the New World, would have been among the foods introduced about this time. The Europeans, having virtually exterminated the Arawaks, introduced slave labor to work in the plantations and over the years millions of Africans were brought to the islands. The slaves were forbidden to raise cattle and frequently prevented from eating fresh fish or meat, so they came to depend on salted fish. They acquired a great liking for it and salt cod has remained popular, inspite of the availability of so much fresh fish.

Although the Africans were initially not allowed their traditional foods, yams, okra and ackee were later brought from Africa. They retained their traditional cooking style and were renowned for their culinary skills.

For most slaves, their diet was bland and monotonous and it was they who made the most of the island's pungent spices and seasonings to flavor their broths and stews. When slavery was abolished in 1830, plantation owners looked elsewhere for labor and found it among people from the Middle East, India and China. They came as indentured laborers and traders and

Picking out the perfect ingredient from a market stall in Martinique (below) or from trays heaped with chilies (right).

brought with them a wealth of new customs, cooking styles and foods.

Thus out of this turbulent past comes a cuisine that is colorful and versatile, imaginative and abounding in creativity. My style of cooking acknowledges the roots of our food culture and celebrates the talents of its cooks. The recipes here have been developed using traditional styles and ingredients in contemporary ways. The Caribbean is renowned for its liberal use of spices and herbs, and for marinating and seasoning meat and fish. The waters are a paradise of tropical fish and shellfish, while fresh vegetables, fragrant herbs and spices grow in profusion. Tropical fruits and vegetables are ideal for vegetarians, offering interesting texture and flavor. Yams, sweet potatoes and other staples go well with spicy tomato-based sauces. Okra and pumpkin, when stir-

fried with shell-fish, make delicious, quick and easy lunches, while mangoes and pineapple add that special touch to fruit salads and drinks. Of course, our sugar cane crops produce potent rum that make delicious punches and cocktails which are always enjoyed by visitors to the islands. Our custom is always to have a little something in the fridge or cupboard, such as patties, ice-cold tart, lemonade or luscious ice cream – just in case a visitor or friend pops in. Caribbean families enjoy entertaining at home and prefer it to dining out. Our buffets usually cater for all tastes, including picky children or non-meat eaters. I hope this cookbook will enable you to bring the delights of the Caribbean kitchen to your friends, families and guests and encourage you to create your own tastes of the Caribbean.

INGREDIENTS

The following ingredients are typically used in Caribbean cooking. Some may be unfamiliar, but they are all available in supermarkets and stores selling Caribbean foods. Commercial blends of herbs and spices can be used to season meat and fish, or try a homemade mixture; spice seasoning and herb seasoning.

ACKEE
This is the fruit of an evergreen tree. The texture is soft, resembling scrambled eggs and it has a slightly lemony flavor. Traditionally served with saltfish, it is also delicious with prawns or vegetables. It is available, canned, from Caribbean stores.

EGGPLANT
There are many varieties – large, purple and oval-shaped, small and round, or thin and pale purple. In west Africa, the small, round, white eggplants are known as "garden eggs".

BEANS AND PEAS
These include black-eyed peas, red kidney beans, black beans, pigeon peas (gunga peas) and various colored lentils. They are often combined with rice or used in soups and stews.

Clockwise from top left: cooked jumbo shrimp, salt cod (dried salted cod) red bream, small red snappers and cooked shrimp.

CASSAVA
This tropical root vegetable originated in Brazil, and was introduced to Africa at the beginning of the 17th century. It is a long irregularly shaped root vegetable with a rough brown skin and hard white starchy flesh. A popular vegetable in the West Indies, it can be eaten boiled, baked or fried.

Clockwise from top left: large and small avocados, limes, guavas, pineapple, large mangoes and small mangoes.

CHAYOTE
Also known as christophene or cho-cho, this is a pear-shaped vegetable with a large central pit. It has a bland flavor and is similar in texture to squash. It is cooked and used as a side dish or in soups.

COCONUT
This is a large one-seeded nut of the coconut palm tree. The mature coconut has a hairy outer shell containing sweet thick white flesh, from which coconut milk is extracted. Chop into small pieces then purée with a little water and press through a sieve to extract the milk.

COCONUT MILK
Commercially made, coconut milk can be bought canned or frozen from most supermarkets, grocery and health food stores. It can be stored indefinitely. For use in recipes, skim the cream off the top.

CORNMEAL
Cornmeal is made from dried ground corn kernels. The type most commonly used is yellow – either fine or coarse-grained. Cornmeal can be used to make cakes, breads and hot cereal or as a coating for frying fish or chicken.

DHAL
In the Caribbean dhal refers to a spicy soup made from split peas or lentils. Dhal puri (or roti) is an unleavened bread.

TARO
A small globular root vegetable, related to the dasheen. The flesh is white and starchy like potato and after peeling can either be boiled and served as an accompaniment to stews or in soup.

Clockwise from top left: okra, chayote, baby eggplants, eggplant, garden eggs and ackee.

GREEN BANANAS
Only certain varieties are used in cooking. They are usually boiled, with or without their skins. Widely available in Caribbean stores.

Clockwise from top left: cassava, taro, orange sweet potatoes, white yam and white sweet potatoes.

Clockwise from top left: green plantains, coconut, ripe yellow plantains and green bananas.

GUAVA

The pale yellow edible skin covers rose-pink succulent flesh, which in turn covers a seed-laden soft pulp. Guavas have a slightly spiced smell and are used to make jam and jelly or added to fruit salads.

HERB SEASONING

Pound 4 chopped scallions, 1 garlic clove, 1 tablespoon each fresh, or 1 teaspoon dried, thyme and basil with 1 tablespoon fresh cilantro, in a mortar until smooth.

MANGOES

Mangoes come in a variety of shapes, sizes, colors and textures. Unripe, they are green, turning yellow, pink or crimson-green as they ripen. For desserts, jellies or jams, make sure the fruit is ripe — it should feel pliable to the touch without being too spongy. Unripe, green mangoes are used for chutney, curries and stews.

OKRA

Okra is used widely in Caribbean cookery. Avoid larger varieties and choose small, firm ones. Wash and dry before trimming and cutting to prevent them from getting too sticky.

PEPPERS

The *Capsicum frutescens* family includes hot and sweet peppers and there are many varieties of hot peppers — or chilies. Fresh chilies can be green, red or yellow. The seeds and core are the hottest part and can be removed before use, under cold running water. A wide variety of peppers is grown in the Caribbean. One of the hottest is the "Scotch Bonnet" pepper. It's best to wear gloves when preparing peppers. Take care not to rub your eyes afterwards.

PLANTAINS

These are a member of the banana family. They are inedible raw and must be cooked before eating. They can be green, yellow or very dark according to ripeness and can be roasted, boiled, mashed and fried. Plantains can be eaten as an appetizer, in soups, as a vegetable or in desserts.

SALT COD

Of all the salt fish, cod has the best flavor. To remove the salt, wash well and soak for several hours or overnight in cold water, then remove the fish to clean water and boil for 15–20 minutes. Discard the water. Flake the fish, discarding the skin and bones.

Clockwise from top left: split red lentils, red kidney beans, fresh pigeon peas, cornmeal, dried pigeon peas, yellow split peas and lima beans.

Clockwise from top: red bell pepper, red and orange Scotch Bonnet peppers, small green and red chilies, sweet green bell peppers, Scotch Bonnet peppers and large green and red chilies.

SNAPPER OR RED FISH

A silver, pinkish-red fish with firm white flesh, snapper is imported in small or large sizes from approximately 8 ounces–3 pounds. Snapper can be fried, baked, steamed or boiled.

SPICE SEASONING

Mix 1 tablespoon garlic powder, ½ tablespoon coarse-ground black pepper, ½ tablespoon each paprika, celery salt and curry powder with 1 teaspoon sugar. Store in a dry container.

SWEET POTATO

The skin of this vegetable ranges in color from white to pink to reddish brown. The white-fleshed, red-skinned variety is most commonly used in Caribbean cooking. Sweet potatoes can be boiled, roasted, fried, mashed or baked in their skins — and are used in sweet and savory dishes.

YAM

These come in all sizes — some varieties are huge, so when buying always ask for a piece of the desired size. The flesh is either yellow or white and can be eaten boiled, roasted, baked, mashed or made into chips or fu fu.

SOUPS AND STARTERS

In the Caribbean, soup can be either a starter or a meal in itself. Time and effort is often spent making good rich stocks from meat and fish which become the base for a family meal. However, for a first course, lighter soups, like Creamy Spinach Soup, and Fish and Sweet Potato Soup, are ideal being both simple and tasty. Snacks not only make delicious accompaniments to drinks, they are also excellent as starters or can be served at picnics or parties. Spinach Pastries are my version of the more traditional minced meat patties.

Creamy Spinach Soup

A smooth and luscious soup, so easy that you will make it with delight, over and over.

INGREDIENTS

Serves 4
2 tablespoons butter
1 small onion, chopped
1½ pounds fresh spinach, chopped
5 cups vegetable stock
¼ cup coconut cream
freshly grated nutmeg
1¼ cups light cream
salt and freshly ground black pepper
fresh chopped chives, to garnish

1 Melt the butter in a saucepan over a moderate heat and sauté the onion for a few minutes until soft. Add the spinach, cover the pan and cook gently for 10 minutes, until the spinach has wilted.

2 Pour the spinach mixture into a blender or food processor and add a little of the stock. Blend until smooth.

3 Return mixture to the pan and add the remaining stock, coconut cream, salt, pepper and nutmeg. Simmer for 15 minutes to thicken.

4 Add the cream, stir well and heat through – do not boil. Serve hot, garnished with chives.

—— COOK'S TIP ——

If fresh spinach is not available, use frozen. Milk can be substituted for the cream – in which case, use half stock and half milk.

Beef Broth with Cassava

This simple, tasty "big," soup is almost like a stew. Such soups, made in one pot, are everyday, family fare. The addition of wine is not traditional, but dresses this soup up for a party.

INGREDIENTS

Serves 4

1 pound stewing beef, cubed
5 cups beef stock
1¼ cups medium dry white wine
1 tablespoon brown sugar
1 onion, finely chopped
1 bay leaf
1 bouquet garni
1 thyme sprig
1 tablespoon tomato paste
1 large carrot, sliced
10 ounces cassava or yam, cubed
2 ounces fresh spinach, chopped
a little hot pepper sauce, to taste
salt and freshly ground black pepper

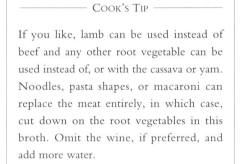

1 Put the beef, stock, wine, sugar, onion, bay leaf, bouquet garni, thyme and tomato paste in a large saucepan, bring to a boil and then cover and simmer for about 1¼ hours.

2 Add the carrot, cassava or yam, spinach, a few drops of hot pepper sauce, salt and pepper and simmer for another 15 minutes until both the meat and vegetables are tender.

---- COOK'S TIP ----

If you like, lamb can be used instead of beef and any other root vegetable can be used instead of, or with the cassava or yam. Noodles, pasta shapes, or macaroni can replace the meat entirely, in which case, cut down on the root vegetables in this broth. Omit the wine, if preferred, and add more water.

Fish and Sweet Potato Soup

The subtle sweetness of the potato combined with the fish and the aromatic flavor of oregano, makes this a very appealing soup.

INGREDIENTS

Serves 4

$\frac{1}{2}$ onion, chopped
6 ounces sweet potato, peeled and diced
6 ounces boneless white fish fillet, skinned
2 ounces carrot, chopped
1 teaspoon fresh chopped oregano or $\frac{1}{2}$ teaspoon dried
$\frac{1}{2}$ teaspoon ground cinnamon
$5\frac{1}{2}$ cups fish stock
5 tablespoons light cream
chopped fresh parsley, to garnish

1 Put the onion, sweet potato, fish, carrot, oregano, cinnamon and half of the stock in a saucepan. Bring to a boil, then simmer for 20 minutes or until the potatoes are cooked.

2 Set the liquid aside to cool, then pour into a blender or food processor and blend until smooth.

3 Return the soup to the saucepan, then add the remaining stock or water and gently bring to a boil. Reduce the heat to low and add the light cream, then gently heat through without boiling. Serve hot, garnished with the chopped parsley.

Caribbean Vegetable Soup

This vegetable soup is refreshing and filling and good as a main course for lunch. Cooked meat and fish can also be added.

INGREDIENTS

Serves 4

2 tablespoons butter or margarine
1 onion, chopped
1 garlic clove, crushed
2 carrots, sliced
$6\frac{1}{4}$ cups vegetable stock or canned broth
2 bay leaves
2 thyme sprigs
1 celery stalk, finely chopped
2 green bananas, peeled and cut into 4
6 ounces white yam or taro, peeled and cubed
2 tablespoons red lentils
1 chayote, peeled and chopped
2 tablespoons macaroni (optional)
salt and freshly ground black pepper
chopped scallion, to garnish

1 Melt the butter or margarine and fry the onion, garlic and carrots for a few minutes, stirring occasionally. Add the stock, bay leaves and thyme and bring to a boil.

2 Add the celery, green bananas, white yam or taro, lentils, chayote and macaroni, if using. Season the soup and simmer for 25 minutes or until the vegetables are cooked. Serve garnished with scallion.

COOK'S TIP

Use other root vegetables or potatoes if yam or taro are not available. Add more stock for a thinner soup.

Split Pea and Pumpkin Soup

Corned beef is often used in this creamy pea soup.

INGREDIENTS

Serves 4

8 ounces split peas, soaked
5 cups water
2 tablespoons butter or margarine
1 onion, finely chopped
8 ounces pumpkin, chopped
3 fresh tomatoes, peeled and chopped
1 teaspoon dried tarragon, crushed
1 tablespoon chopped fresh cilantro
½ teaspoon ground cumin
vegetable stock cube, crumbled
chili powder, to taste
cilantro sprigs, to garnish

1 Soak the split peas overnight in enough water to cover, then drain. Place the split peas in a large saucepan, add the water and boil for about 30 minutes until cooked.

2 In a separate pan, melt the butter or margarine and sauté the onion for a few minutes until soft but not browned.

3 Add the pumpkin, tomatoes, tarragon, cilantro, cumin, stock cube and chili powder and bring to a boil.

4 Stir the vegetable mixture into the cooked split peas and their liquid. Simmer gently for 20 minutes or until the vegetables are tender. If the soup is too thick, add another ⅔ cup of water. Serve hot, garnished with cilantro.

Lamb and Lentil Soup

You could add more vegetables for a "bigger" soup.

INGREDIENTS

Serves 4
6¼ cups water or stock
2 pounds neck of lamb, cut into chops
½ onion, chopped
1 garlic clove, crushed
1 bay leaf
1 clove
2 thyme sprigs
8 ounces potatoes
6 ounces red lentils
2½ cups water
salt and freshly ground black pepper
parsley, to garnish

1 Put the water and meat in a large saucepan with the onion, garlic, bay leaf, clove and thyme sprigs. Bring to a boil and simmer for about 1 hour, until the lamb is tender.

2 Cut the potatoes into 1-inch pieces and add to the pan.

3 Add the lentils to the pan and season the soup with a little salt and plenty of black pepper.

4 Add 1¼ cups water or more if the soup becomes too thick, to come just above the surface of the meat and vegetables. Cover and simmer for 25 minutes or until the lentils are cooked and well blended into the soup. Just before serving, sprinkle in the parsley and stir well.

Spinach Pastries

INGREDIENTS

Makes 10–12
For the pastry
2 cups flour
½ cup butter or margarine, chilled and
    diced
1 egg yolk
milk, to glaze

For the filling
2 tablespoons butter or margarine
1 small onion, finely chopped
6–8 ounces fresh leaf
    spinach, chopped
½ teaspoon ground cumin
½ vegetable stock cube, crumbled
freshly ground black pepper

1 Preheat the oven to 400°F. Lightly grease the hollows of a muffin pan.

2 First make the spinach filling. Melt the butter or margarine in a saucepan, add the onion and cook gently until softened. Stir in the spinach, then add the cumin, stock cube and pepper and cook for 5 minutes or until the spinach has wilted. Set aside to cool.

3 To make the pastry, put the flour in a large bowl and rub in the butter or margarine, until the mixture resembles fine bread crumbs. Add the egg yolk and 2–3 tablespoons cold water and mix to a firm dough. Turn out the pastry on to a floured surface.

4 Knead for a few seconds, divide the dough in half and roll out one half to a square or rectangle. Cut out 10–12 rounds using a 3½-inch pastry cutter. Press into the hollows of the prepared pan. Spoon about 1 tablespoon of the spinach mixture into the pastry cases.

5 Roll out the remaining dough and cut out slightly smaller rounds to cover the pastries. Press the edges with a fork, to seal. Prick the tops with the fork. Brush with milk and bake for 15–20 minutes until golden brown. Serve hot or cold.

Salt Cod Fritters (Stamp and Go)

These delicious fritters are also known as Accras.

INGREDIENTS

Makes 15
1 cup self-rising flour
1 cup flour
½ teaspoon baking powder
6 ounces soaked salt cod, shredded
1 egg, beaten
1 tablespoon chopped scallion
1 garlic clove, crushed
½ teaspoon freshly ground black
    pepper
½ hot chili pepper, seeded and finely
    chopped
¼ teaspoon turmeric (optional)
3 tablespoons milk
vegetable oil, for shallow frying

1 Sift the flours and baking powder together into a bowl, then add the salt cod, egg, scallion, garlic, pepper, hot pepper and turmeric, if using. Add a little of the milk and mix well.

2 Gradually stir in the remaining milk, adding just enough to make a thick batter. Stir thoroughly so that all ingredients are completely combined.

3 Heat a little oil in a large frying pan until very hot. Add spoonfuls of the mixture and fry for a few minutes on each side until golden brown and puffed. Lift out the fritters, drain on paper towels and keep warm while cooking the rest of the mixture in the same way. Serve the fritters hot or cold, as a snack, or hors d'oeuvres.

Stuffed Eggs

Ideal as a snack for a cocktail party or as a first course. A variety of fillings can be used instead of cheese, such as canned sardines or tuna.

INGREDIENTS

Serves 4–6
6 eggs
1 tablespoon mayonnaise
2 tablespoons grated Cheddar cheese
½ teaspoon white pepper
2 teaspoons chopped fresh chives
2 radishes, thinly sliced, to garnish

1 Cook the eggs for about 10 minutes until hard-boiled. Set aside the eggs to cool in cold water, then remove the shells.

2 Cut the eggs in half and place the egg yolks in a small bowl with the mayonnaise, cheese, pepper and chives.

3 Mash together with a fork until well blended.

4 Fill the whites with the egg and cheese mixture, and garnish with thinly sliced radishes.

Crab Cakes

These are delicious and they're just as good made with canned tunafish, too.

INGREDIENTS

Makes about 15
8 ounces white crab meat
4 ounces cooked potatoes, mashed
2 tablespoons fresh herb seasoning
½ teaspoon mild mustard
½ teaspoon freshly ground black pepper
½ hot chili pepper
1 tablespoon shrimp paste (optional)
½ teaspoon dried oregano, crushed
1 egg, beaten
flour, for dusting
oil, for frying
lime wedges and basil leaves, to garnish

For the tomato salsa
1 tablespoon butter or margarine
½ onion, finely chopped
2 canned plum tomatoes, chopped
1 garlic clove, crushed
⅔ cup water
1–2 teaspoons malt vinegar
1 tablespoon chopped fresh cilantro
½ hot chili pepper, chopped

1 To make the crab cakes, mix together the crab meat, potatoes, herb seasoning, mustard, peppers, shrimp paste, if using, oregano and egg in a large bowl. Chill for 30 minutes.

2 Make the tomato salsa. Melt the butter or margarine in a small pan.

3 Add the onion, tomato and garlic and sauté for about 5 minutes until the onion is soft. Add the water, vinegar, cilantro and hot pepper. Simmer for 10 minutes and then blend to a smooth paste in a food processor or blender and pour into a bowl. Keep warm or chill as desired.

4 Using a spoon, shape the mixture into rounds and dust with flour. Heat a little oil in a frying pan and fry the crab cakes a few at a time for 2–3 minutes on each side until golden brown. Drain and keep warm while cooking the remaining cakes. Serve with the warm or cold tomato salsa, and garnish with lime wedges and basil leaves.

Plantain and Sweet Potato Chips

INGREDIENTS

Serves 4
2 green plantains
1 small sweet potato
oil, for deep-frying
salt

1 Using a small sharp knife, remove top and bottom of the plantains and cut in half. Make three or four slits lengthways along the natural ridge of the plantains and lift away the skin. Place the plantains in a bowl of cold salted water.

2 Peel the sweet potato under cold running water, and add to the bowl of salted water.

3 Heat the oil in a large saucepan or deep-fat fryer. While the oil is heating, remove the vegetables one at a time from the salted water, pat dry on paper towels and slice into thin rounds with a sharp knife or vegetable slicer.

VARIATION

For maximum crispness, only green plantains should be used. If these are not available, green bananas can be used instead and yam is a good substitute for sweet potatoes. All of the vegetables should be soaked in cold salted water to prevent discoloration.

4 Fry the plantains and sweet potatoes until crisp, then drain and transfer to a dish lined with paper towels. Sprinkle with salt and cool.

Coconut Jumbo Shrimp

INGREDIENTS

Serves 3–4
12 large raw shrimp
2 garlic cloves, crushed
1 tablespoon lemon juice
4 tablespoons fine coconut
2 tablespoons snipped fresh chives
²⁄₃ cup milk
2 eggs, beaten
salt and freshly ground black pepper
oil, for deep frying
lime or lemon slices or wedges and
   Italian parsley, to garnish

COOK'S TIP

If large raw shrimp are difficult to obtain, substitute cooked shrimp. However, the raw shrimp will absorb more flavor from the marinade, so they are the ideal choice.

1 Shell and devein the shrimp, leaving the tails intact, then cut the shrimp along the length of their backs without cutting through and fan them out. Rinse under cold water and pat dry.

2 Blend together the garlic, lemon juice and seasoning in a shallow dish, then add the shrimp and marinate for about 1 hour.

3 Mix together the coconut and chives in a shallow dish, and put the milk and eggs in two separate dishes. Dip each shrimp into the milk, then into the beaten egg and finally into the coconut and chive mixture.

4 Heat the oil in a large saucepan or deep-fat fryer and fry the shrimp for about 1 minute, until golden. Drain on paper towels and serve hot, garnished with the lime or lemon slices and parsley.

Vegetarian Dishes and Salads

*Vegetarians will find they have much to choose
from in the Caribbean and all cooks will enjoy
the creative scope that the choice of vegetables
and beans provide. Tropical vegetables are usually
available here all year round in this country
although you may need to shop around and they
will not be as plentiful or as inexpensive as in
the Caribbean. Some of the recipes in this
section are my version of best-loved international
dishes which are also cooked in the Caribbean,
such as Chow Mein, Red Bean Chili,
and Macaroni and Cheese.*

Spicy Potato Salad

This tasty salad is quick to prepare, and makes a satisfying accompaniment to grilled or barbecued meat or fish.

INGREDIENTS

Serves 6

2 pounds potatoes, peeled
2 red bell peppers
2 celery stalks
1 shallot
2 or 3 scallions
1 green chili, finely chopped
1 garlic clove, crushed
2 teaspoons finely chopped
   fresh chives
2 teaspoons finely chopped
   fresh basil
1 tablespoon finely chopped fresh
   parsley
1 tablespoon light cream
3 tablespoons mayonnaise
1 teaspoon mild mustard
½ tablespoon sugar
chopped fresh chives, to garnish

1 Boil the potatoes until tender but still firm. Drain and cool, then cut into 1-inch cubes and place in a large salad bowl.

2 Halve the peppers, cut away and discard the core and seeds and cut into small pieces. Finely chop the celery, shallot, and scallions and slice the chili very thinly, discarding the seeds. Add the vegetables to the cubed potatoes together with the garlic and chopped herbs.

3 Blend together the cream, mayonnaise, mustard and sugar in a small bowl, stirring until the mixture is well combined.

4 Pour the dressing over the potato and vegetable salad and stir gently to coat evenly. Serve, garnished with the chopped chives.

Mango, Tomato and Red Onion Salad

This salad makes an appetizing first course, the underripe mango has a subtle sweetness and the flavor blends well with the tomato.

INGREDIENTS

Serves 4
1 firm underripe mango
2 large tomatoes or 1 beefsteak tomato, sliced
½ red onion, sliced into rings
½ cucumber, peeled and thinly sliced
2 tablespoons sunflower or vegetable oil
1 tablespoon lemon juice
1 garlic clove, crushed
½ teaspoon hot pepper sauce
salt and freshly ground black pepper
sugar, to taste
fresh chopped chives, to garnish

1 Cut away two thick slices either side of the mango pit and cut into slices. Peel the skin from the slices.

2 Arrange the mango, tomato, onion and cucumber slices on a large serving plate.

3 Blend the oil, lemon juice, garlic, hot pepper sauce, salt and black pepper in a blender or food processor, or place in a small jar and shake vigorously. Add a pinch of sugar to taste and mix again.

4 Pour the dressing over the salad and garnish with chopped chives.

Spinach Plantain Rounds

This delectable way of serving plantains is a little fussy to make, but well worth it! The plantains must be ripe, but still firm.

INGREDIENTS

Serves 4
2 large ripe plantains
oil, for frying
2 tablespoons butter or margarine
2 tablespoons finely chopped onion
2 garlic cloves, crushed
1 pound fresh spinach, chopped
pinch of freshly grated nutmeg
1 egg, beaten
whole wheat flour, for dusting
salt and freshly ground black pepper

1 Using a small sharp knife, carefully cut each plantain lengthwise into four slices.

2 Heat a little oil in a large frying pan and fry the plantain slices on both sides until light golden brown but not fully cooked. Drain on paper towels and reserve the oil.

3 Melt the butter or margarine in a saucepan and sauté the onion and garlic for a few minutes until the onion is soft. Add the spinach, salt, pepper and nutmeg. Cover and cook for about 5 minutes until the spinach has wilted. Cool, then turn into a strainer and press out any excess moisture.

4 Curl the plantain slices into rings and secure each ring with half a wooden toothpick. Pack each ring with a little of the spinach mixture.

5 Place the egg and flour in two separate shallow dishes. Add a little more oil to the frying pan if necessary and heat until moderately hot. Dip the plantain rings in the egg and then in the flour and fry on both sides for 1–2 minutes until golden brown. Drain on paper towels and serve hot or cold with a salad, or as part of a dinner.

COOK'S TIP

If fresh spinach is not available, use frozen spinach, thawed and drained. The plantain rings can be small or large, and if preferred ground meat, fish or beans can be used instead of spinach for the filling.

Peppery Bean Salad

This pretty salad uses canned beans for speed and convenience.

INGREDIENTS

Serves 4–6
15-ounce can kidney beans, drained
15-ounce can black-eyed peas, drained
15-ounce can chick-peas, drained
¼ red bell pepper
¼ green bell pepper
6 radishes
1 tablespoon chopped scallion
1 teaspoon ground cumin
1 tablespoon tomato ketchup
2 tablespoons olive oil
1 tablespoon white wine vinegar
1 garlic clove, crushed
½ teaspoon hot pepper sauce
salt
sliced scallion, to garnish

1 Drain the canned beans and chick-peas and rinse under cold running water. Shake off the excess water and turn them into a large salad bowl.

2 Core, seed and chop the peppers. Trim the radishes and slice thinly. Add to the beans with the pepper and scallion.

3 Mix together the cumin, ketchup, oil, vinegar and garlic in a small bowl. Add a little salt and hot pepper sauce to taste and stir again thoroughly.

4 Pour the dressing over the salad and mix. Chill for at least 1 hour before serving, garnished with scallion.

COOK'S TIP

For an even tastier salad, allow the ingredients to marinate for a few hours.

Pigeon Peas, Chayote and Pumpkin Stew

INGREDIENTS

Serves 2–3

2 tablespoons butter or margarine
1 onion, chopped
2 garlic cloves, crushed
2 carrots, sliced
4 ounces seeded, peeled pumpkin, chopped
1 chayote, peeled, pitted and chopped
4 ounces pigeon peas
2½ cups rich vegetable stock
2 thyme sprigs
1 tablespoon fresh cilantro leaves
¼ cup coconut cream
½ teaspoon ground cinnamon
hot pepper
salt
chopped fresh cilantro, to garnish

1 Melt the butter or margarine in a large saucepan and sauté the onion and garlic for a few minutes until the onion is soft.

2 Stir in the carrots, pumpkin, chayote, pigeon peas, stock and thyme. Bring to a boil, then reduce the heat and simmer for 10 minutes.

3 Add the cilantro, coconut cream, cinnamon, hot pepper and salt. Simmer until the vegetables are tender and the sauce is reduced and thick. Serve hot, garnished with cilantro.

— COOK'S TIP —

If chayote is not available, use zucchini or marrow instead. Canned beans or peas can be substituted for the pigeon peas.

Ackee with Mushrooms

Ackee or akee is a fruit with a soft texture and a slight lemony flavor.

INGREDIENTS

Serves 4

2 tablespoons butter or margarine
2 tablespoons vegetable oil
1 onion, chopped
2 garlic cloves, crushed
2 canned plum tomatoes plus
    2 tablespoons of the tomato juice
½ red pepper, chopped
1 hot chili pepper, chopped (optional)
1¾ cups mushrooms, chopped
1-pound 6-ounce can ackee, drained
1 tablespoon chopped fresh parsley
⅔ cup vegetable stock
salt
chopped fresh parsley and cilantro
    sprigs, to garnish

1 Heat the butter or margarine and oil in a large frying pan, add the onion and garlic and sauté for a few minutes over a moderate heat until the onion has softened.

2 Add the canned tomatoes, tomato juice, red pepper, hot chili pepper if using, mushrooms, ackee, parsley, stock and salt to taste.

3 Stir gently and slowly bring to the boil, then reduce the heat and simmer for 5 minutes. Serve with rice or boiled green bananas. Garnish with parsley and cilantro.

— COOK'S TIP —

Use a metal spoon or fork and carefully mix, as ackee breaks up easily. Ackee adds a subtle flavor to most vegetables, beans or peas.

Macaroni Cheese Pie

INGREDIENTS

Serves 4

8 ounces macaroni
2 tablespoons butter or margarine
3 tablespoons flour
2 cups milk
1 teaspoon mild mustard
½ teaspoon ground cinnamon
6 ounces mature Cheddar cheese, grated
1 egg, beaten
1 tablespoon butter or margarine
⅓ cup chopped scallions
3 tablespoons canned chopped
  tomatoes
4 ounces corn
freshly ground black pepper
chopped fresh parsley, to garnish

1 Heat the oven to 350°F. Cook the macaroni in boiling salted water for 10 minutes until just tender. Drain thoroughly, then rinse under cold water and drain again.

2 Melt the butter or margarine in a saucepan and stir in the flour to make a roux. Slowly pour in the milk, whisking constantly, and simmer gently for 5–10 minutes.

3 Add the mustard, cinnamon and 4 ounces of the cheese and cook gently, stirring frequently, then remove from the heat and whisk in the egg. Set aside and make the filling.

4 To make the filling, heat the butter or margarine in a small frying pan and cook the scallions, chopped plum tomatoes and corn over a gentle heat for 5–10 minutes.

5 Put half the cooked macaroni in a greased ovenproof dish. Pour over half the cheese sauce and mix well, then spoon the tomato and corn mixture over the macaroni.

6 Put the remaining macaroni into the saucepan with the remaining sauce, stir well and then spread the macaroni and sauce carefully over the tomato and corn mixture.

7 Top with the remaining grated cheese and bake in the oven for about 45 minutes, or until the top is golden and bubbly. If possible let the pie stand for 30 minutes before serving. Serve hot, garnished with the chopped fresh parsley.

Red Bean Chili

This vegetarian chili can be adapted to accommodate meat eaters by adding either ground beef or lamb in place of the lentils. Add the meat once the onions are soft and fry until well-browned before adding the tomatoes.

INGREDIENTS

Serves 4

2 tablespoons vegetable oil
1 onion, chopped
14-ounce can chopped tomatoes
2 garlic cloves, crushed
1¼ cups white wine
1¼ cups vegetable stock
4 ounces red lentils
2 thyme sprigs or 1 teaspoon dried thyme
2 teaspoons ground cumin
3 tablespoons dark soy sauce
½ hot chili pepper, finely chopped
1 teaspoon five-spice powder
1 tablespoon oyster sauce (optional)
8-ounce can red kidney beans, drained
2 teaspoons sugar
salt

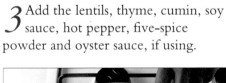

1 Heat the oil in a large saucepan and fry the onion over a moderate heat for a few minutes until slightly softened.

2 Add the tomatoes and garlic, cook for 10 minutes, then stir in the wine and stock.

3 Add the lentils, thyme, cumin, soy sauce, hot pepper, five-spice powder and oyster sauce, if using.

4 Cover and simmer for 40 minutes or until the lentils are cooked, stirring occasionally and adding more water if the lentils begin to dry out.

5 Stir in the kidney beans and sugar and continue cooking for about 10 minutes, adding extra stock or water if necessary. Season to taste with salt and serve hot with boiled rice.

COOK'S TIP

Fiery chilies can irritate the skin, so always wash your hands well after handling them and take care not to touch your eyes. If you like really hot, spicy food, then add the seeds from the chili, too.

Spicy Vegetable Chow Mein

Chow Mein is popular in Guyana, where it is usually made with shredded chicken or shrimp. This vegetarian version can be adapted to suit all tastes.

INGREDIENTS

Serves 3

8 ounces egg noodles
2–3 tablespoons vegetable oil
2 garlic cloves, crushed
1 onion, chopped
4 ounces each red and green bell
   pepper, chopped
4 ounces green beans, blanched
3 tablespoons finely chopped celery
½ teaspoon five-spice powder
1 vegetable stock cube, crumbled
½ teaspoon freshly ground black pepper
1 tablespoon soy sauce (optional)
salt

1 Cook the noodles in plenty of boiling salted water for 10 minutes or according to the package instructions, then drain and spread out to cool, on a large plate.

2 Heat the oil in a wok or large frying pan and stir-fry the garlic, onion, red and green peppers, green beans and celery, tossing them together to mix.

3 Add the five-spice powder, the stock cube and black pepper, stir well and cook for 5 minutes.

4 Stir in the noodles and soy sauce, if using and season with salt. Serve.

--- COOK'S TIP ---

Shredded omelet or sliced hard-boiled eggs are also popular garnishes, and Tuna Chow Mein is a children's favorite.

Eggplant Stuffed with Sweet Potato

INGREDIENTS

Serves 3–4

8 ounces sweet potatoes, peeled
½ teaspoon chopped fresh thyme
3 ounces Cheddar cheese, diced
2 tablespoons chopped scallions
1 tablespoon each chopped, red and
   green bell pepper
1 garlic clove, crushed
2 large eggplants
2 tablespoons flour
1 tablespoon spice seasoning
olive oil, for frying
2 tomatoes, sliced
salt and freshly ground black pepper
chopped fresh parsley, to garnish

1 Preheat the oven to 350°F. Cook the sweet potatoes until tender, then drain, place in a bowl and mash thoroughly until smooth.

2 Add the thyme, cheese, scallions, red and green peppers, garlic and salt and pepper and mix.

3 Cut each eggplant lengthwise into four slices. Mix the flour and spice seasoning on a plate and dust over each eggplant slice.

4 Heat a little oil in a frying pan and fry the eggplant until browned, but not fully cooked. Drain and cool. Spoon a little of the potato mixture into the middle of each eggplant slice and roll up.

5 Butter two large pieces of foil and place four rolls on each. Add slices of tomato, wrap up the packages and bake for 20 minutes. Serve hot, garnished with parsley.

FISH AND SEAFOOD

With its thousands of miles of shoreline, it's not surprising that fish plays an important part in Caribbean cookery. The recipes collected here include several traditional dishes, like Ackee and Salt Cod, and Eschovished Fish, as well as others I've created myself which have a more contemporary flavor. In Caribbean recipes fish is always seasoned with herbs and spices and is either marinated, cooked or served with fresh lime juice or lemon juice. If the fresh fish you require is not available, then look out for frozen fish, available in many Caribbean stores.

Creole Fish Stew

A simple attractive dish – good for a dinner party.

INGREDIENTS

Serves 4–6
2 whole porgies or large snapper, prepared and cut into 1-inch pieces
2 tablespoons spice seasoning
2 tablespoons malt vinegar
flour, for dusting
oil, for frying

For the sauce
2 tablespoons vegetable oil
1 tablespoon butter or margarine
1 onion, finely chopped
10 ounces fresh tomatoes, peeled and finely chopped
2 garlic cloves, crushed
2 thyme sprigs
2½ cups fish stock or water
½ teaspoon ground cinnamon
1 hot chili pepper, chopped
4 ounces each red and green bell pepper, finely chopped
salt
oregano sprigs, to garnish

1 Sprinkle the fish with the spice seasoning and vinegar, turning to coat. Set aside to marinate for at least 2 hours or overnight in the fridge.

2 When ready to cook, place a little flour on a large plate and coat the fish pieces, shaking off any excess flour.

3 Heat a little oil in a large frying pan and fry the fish pieces for about 5 minutes until golden brown, then set aside. Don't worry if the fish is not cooked through, it will finish cooking in the sauce.

4 To make the sauce, heat the oil and butter or margarine in a large frying pan or wok and stir-fry the onion for 5 minutes. Add the tomatoes, garlic and thyme, stir well and simmer for another 5 minutes. Stir in the stock or water, cinnamon and hot pepper.

5 Add the fish pieces and the chopped peppers. Simmer until the fish is cooked through, and the stock has reduced to a thick sauce. Adjust the seasoning with salt. Serve hot, garnished with oregano.

Ackee and Salt Cod

This is a classic of Jamaican cuisine, popular in the Caribbean, served with boiled green bananas.

INGREDIENTS

Serves 4

1 pound salt cod
2 tablespoons butter or margarine
2 tablespoons vegetable oil
1 onion, chopped
2 garlic cloves, crushed
8 ounces chopped fresh tomatoes
½ hot chili pepper, chopped (optional)
½ teaspoon freshly ground black pepper
½ teaspoon dried thyme
½ teaspoon ground allspice
2 tablespoons chopped scallions
1-pound 6-ounce can ackee, drained
Fried Dumplings, to serve

1 Place the salt cod in a bowl and cover with cold water. Leave it to soak for at least 12 hours, changing the water two or three times. Discard the water and rinse in fresh cold water.

2 Put the salt cod in a large saucepan of cold water, bring to a boil, then remove the fish and allow to cool on a plate. Remove and discard the skin and bones, then flake the fish and set aside.

3 Heat the butter or margarine and oil in a large heavy frying pan over a moderate heat. Add the onion and garlic and sauté for 5 minutes. Add the tomatoes and hot chili pepper, if using, and cook gently for another 5 minutes.

4 Add the salt cod, black pepper, thyme, allspice and scallions, stir to mix, then stir in the ackee, taking care not to crush them. If you prefer a moister dish, add a little water or stock. Serve hot with Fried Dumplings.

Salmon in Mango and Ginger Sauce

Mango and salmon complement each other, especially with the subtle flavor of tarragon.

INGREDIENTS

Serves 2
2 salmon steaks (about 10 ounces each)
a little lemon juice
1 or 2 garlic cloves, crushed
1 teaspoon dried tarragon, crushed
2 shallots, coarsely chopped
1 tomato, coarsely chopped
1 ripe mango (about 6 ounces of flesh), chopped
²⁄₃ cup fish stock or water
1 tablespoon ginger syrup
2 tablespoons butter
salt and freshly ground black pepper

1 Place the salmon steaks in a shallow dish and season with the lemon juice, garlic, tarragon and salt and pepper. Set aside in the fridge to marinate for at least 1 hour.

2 Meanwhile, place the shallots, tomato and mango in a blender or food processor and blend until smooth. Add the fish stock or water and the ginger syrup, blend again and set aside.

3 Melt the butter in a frying pan and sauté the salmon steaks for about 5 minutes on each side.

4 Add the mango purée, cover and simmer until salmon is cooked.

5 Transfer the salmon to warmed serving plates. Heat the sauce through, adjust the seasoning and pour over the salmon. Serve hot.

Fried Snapper with Avocado

Caribbean fried fish is often eaten with Fried Dumplings or hard-dough bread, and, as in this recipe, is sometimes accompanied by avocado – it makes a delicious light supper or lunch.

INGREDIENTS

Serves 4
1 lemon
4 red snappers, about 8 ounces each, prepared
2 teaspoons spice seasoning
flour, for dusting
oil, for frying
2 avocados and sliced corn-on-the-cob, to serve
chopped fresh parsley and lime slices, to garnish

1 Squeeze the lemon juice both inside and outside the fish and sprinkle them all over with the spice seasoning. Set the fish aside in a shallow dish to marinate in a cool place for a few hours.

2 Lift the fish out of the dish and dust thoroughly with the flour, shaking off the excess.

3 Heat the oil in a nonstick pan over a moderate heat. Add the fish and fry for about 10 minutes on each side until browned and crisp.

4 Halve the avocados, remove the pits and cut in half again. Peel away the skin and cut the avocado flesh into thin strips.

5 Place the fish on warmed serving plates with the avocado and corn slices. Serve hot, garnished with parsley and lime slices.

Fillets of Trout in Wine Sauce with Plantains

Tropical fish would add a distinctive flavor to this dish, but any filleted white fish can be cooked in this way.

INGREDIENTS

Serves 4
4 trout fillets
spice seasoning, for dusting
2 tablespoons butter or margarine
1 or 2 garlic cloves
²/₃ cup white wine
²/₃ cup fish stock
2 teaspoons honey
1–2 tablespoons chopped fresh parsley
1 yellow plantain
salt and freshly ground black pepper
oil, for frying

1 Season the trout fillets with the spice seasoning and marinate for 1 hour.

COOK'S TIP

Plantains belong to the banana family and can be green, yellow, or brown, depending on ripeness. Unlike bananas, plantains must be cooked. Their subtle flavor works well in spicy dishes.

2 Melt the butter or margarine in a large frying pan and heat gently for 1 minute. Add the fillets and sauté for about 5 minutes, until cooked through, turning carefully once. Transfer to a plate and keep warm.

3 Add the wine, fish stock and honey to the pan, bring to a boil and simmer to reduce slightly. Return the fillets to the pan and spoon over the sauce. Sprinkle with parsley and simmer gently for a few minutes.

4 Meanwhile, peel the plantain, and cut into rounds. Heat a little oil in a frying pan and fry the plantain slices for a few minutes, until golden, turning once. Transfer the fish to serving plates, stir the sauce, adjust the seasoning and pour over the fish. Garnish with the fried plantain.

Eschovished Fish

This dish is of Spanish origin and is very popular throughout the Caribbean. There are as many variations of the name of the dish as there are ways of preparing it.

INGREDIENTS

Serves 4–6
2 pounds red snapper fillet
½ lemon
1 tablespoon spice seasoning
flour, for dusting
oil, for frying
lemon wedges, to garnish

For the sauce
2 tablespoons vegetable oil
1 onion, sliced
½ red bell pepper, sliced
½ chayote, peeled and seeded, cut into small pieces
2 garlic cloves, crushed
½ cup malt vinegar
5 tablespoons water
½ teaspoon ground allspice
1 bay leaf
1 small Scotch Bonnet pepper, chopped
1 tablespoon brown sugar
salt and freshly ground black pepper

1 Place the fish in a shallow dish, squeeze over the lemon, then sprinkle with the spice seasoning and pat into the fish. Let marinate in a cool place for at least 1 hour.

2 Cut the fish into 3-inch pieces and dust with a little flour, shaking off the excess.

3 Heat the oil in a heavy frying pan and fry the fish pieces for 2–3 minutes until golden brown and crisp, turning occasionally. To make the sauce, heat the oil in a heavy frying pan and fry the onion until soft.

4 Add the pepper, chayote and garlic and stir-fry for 2 minutes. Pour in the vinegar, then add the remaining ingredients and simmer gently for 5 minutes. Let stand for 10 minutes, then pour over the fish. Serve hot, garnished with lemon wedges.

COOK'S TIP

In the Caribbean, whole fish are used for this dish but fillets are also fine.

Jumbo Shrimp in Corn Sauce

This sauce makes a hearty filling for baked sweet potatoes.

INGREDIENTS

Serves 4
24–30 large raw shrimp, shelled
spice seasoning, for dusting
juice of 1 lemon
2 tablespoons butter or margarine
1 onion, chopped
2 garlic cloves, crushed
2 tablespoons tomato paste
½ teaspoon dried thyme
½ teaspoon ground cinnamon
1 tablespoon chopped fresh cilantro
½ hot chili pepper, chopped
6 ounces frozen or canned corn
1¼ cups coconut milk
chopped fresh cilantro, to garnish

1 Sprinkle the shrimp with spice seasoning and lemon juice and marinate in a cool place for an hour.

2 Melt the butter or margarine in a saucepan, fry the onion and garlic for 5 minutes, until slightly softened. Add the shrimp and cook for a few minutes, stirring occasionally until cooked through and pink.

3 Transfer the shrimp, onion and garlic to a bowl, leaving behind some of the buttery liquid. Add the tomato paste and cook over a low heat, stirring well. Add the thyme, cinnamon, cilantro and hot pepper and stir well.

4 Blend the corn (reserving about 1 tablespoon) in a blender or food processor with the coconut milk. Add to the pan and simmer until reduced. Add the shrimp and reserved corn, and simmer for 5 minutes. Serve hot, garnished with cilantro.

—— COOK'S TIP ——

If you use raw jumbo shrimp, make a stock from the shells and use in place of some of the coconut milk.

Shrimp and Salt Cod with Okra

An unusual mix of salt cod and shrimp, enhanced by the okra.

INGREDIENTS

Serves 4
1 pound raw shrimp, peeled and deveined
1 tablespoon spice seasoning
2 tablespoons butter or margarine
1 tablespoon olive oil
2 shallots, finely chopped
1 garlic clove, crushed
12 ounces okra, and cut into 1-inch lengths
1 teaspoon curry powder
1 teaspoon shrimp paste
2 tablespoons chopped fresh cilantro
1 tablespoon lemon juice
6 ounces prepared salt cod (see Cook's Tip), shredded

1 Season the shrimp with the spice seasoning and let marinate in a cool place for about 1 hour.

2 Heat the butter or margarine and olive oil in a large frying pan or wok over a moderate heat and stir-fry the shallots and garlic for 5 minutes. Add the okra, curry powder and shrimp paste, stir well and cook for about 10 minutes, until the okra is tender.

3 Add 2 tablespoons water, cilantro, lemon juice, shrimp and salt cod, and cook gently for 5–10 minutes. Adjust the seasoning and serve hot.

—— COOK'S TIP ——

Soak the salt fish for 12 hours, changing the water two or three times. Rinse, bring to a boil in fresh water, then cool.

Crab and Corn Gumbo

INGREDIENTS

Serves 4

2 tablespoons butter or margarine
2 tablespoons flour
1 tablespoon vegetable oil
1 onion, finely chopped
4 ounces okra, trimmed and chopped
2 garlic cloves, crushed
1 tablespoon finely chopped celery
2½ cups fish stock
⅔ cup sherry
1 tablespoon tomato ketchup
½ teaspoon dried oregano
¼ teaspoons allspice
2 teaspoons Worcestershire sauce
hot pepper, to taste
2 ears corn-on-the-cob, chopped
1 pound crab claws
fresh cilantro, to garnish

1 Melt the butter or margarine in a large saucepan over a low heat, add the flour and stir together to make a roux. Cook for about 10 minutes, stirring constantly, to prevent burning, while the roux turns golden brown and then darkens. Turn the roux on to a plate and set aside.

2 Heat the oil in the same saucepan over a moderate heat, add the onion, okra, garlic and celery and stir to mix together. Cook for a few minutes, then add the stock, sherry, ketchup, oregano, allspice, Worcestershire sauce and hot pepper.

3 Bring to a boil, then simmer gently for about 10 minutes until the vegetables are tender. Add the roux, stirring it well into the sauce and cook for a few minutes until thickened.

4 Add the corn and crab claws and continue to simmer gently over a low heat for about 10 minutes until the crab and corn are cooked.

5 Spoon the gumbo into warmed serving plates and garnish with sprigs of fresh cilantro.

Pumpkin and Shrimp with Dried Shrimp

INGREDIENTS

Serves 4

2 ounces dried shrimp
2 tablespoons vegetable or
    sunflower oil
2 tablespoons butter or margarine
1 red onion, chopped
1¾ pounds pumpkin, peeled and
    chopped
8 ounces cooked, shelled shrimp
½ teaspoon ground cinnamon
½ teaspoon five-spice powder
2 garlic cloves, chopped
2 fresh tomatoes, chopped
chopped fresh parsley and lime wedges,
    to garnish

1 Rinse the dried shrimp under cold water and then soak them, in enough hot water to cover, for 35 minutes.

2 Heat the oil and butter or margarine in a large frying pan over a moderate heat. Add the onion and sauté for 5 minutes or until soft.

3 Add the pumpkin and cook for 5–6 minutes, until the pumpkin is slightly tender. Add the shelled shrimp and the dried shrimp together with their soaking water. Stir in the cinnamon, five-spice powder and the chopped garlic.

4 Add the tomatoes and cook over a gentle heat, stirring occasionally, until the pumpkin is soft.

5 Spoon onto a warmed serving plate and serve hot, garnished with the chopped parsley.

MEAT AND POULTRY

Caribbean Mutton Curry, Barbecued Jerk
Chicken, Pork Roasted with Herbs, Spices and
Rum, and Spicy Fried Chicken are
traditional favorites in the Caribbean and are
eaten at festivals, celebrations and at big
family get-togethers.
Along with these recipes, I've also included
newly created recipes such as Thyme and Lime
Chicken, and Peanut Chicken which are simple
and quick, yet have an authentic Caribbean taste.
Many meat dishes originate from Africa and
the meat is cooked with vegetables and
beans, while the ever-popular chicken
can be served in a variety of ways.

Hearty Beef Stew

The dark ale gives this beef stew a real kick. Vary the amount to suit your taste.

INGREDIENTS

Serves 4

2 ounces black-eyed peas
2 tablespoons butter or margarine
1 onion, chopped
1½ pounds stewing beef, cubed
1 teaspoon paprika
2 garlic cloves, crushed
2 teaspoons ground cinnamon
2 teaspoons sugar
2½ cups beef stock
⅔ cup dark ale
3 tablespoons evaporated milk
salt and freshly ground black pepper
baby pattypan squash, steamed, to serve

1 Soak the black-eyed peas overnight, then place in a large saucepan, cover with water and bring to a boil. Boil rapidly for a few minutes, then reduce the heat and simmer for about 30 minutes or until the beans are cooked and tender but still quite firm. Drain the beans, reserving the cooking liquid.

2 Meanwhile, melt the butter or margarine in a large saucepan and sauté the onion for a few minutes. Add the beef, paprika, garlic, cinnamon and sugar and fry for about 5 minutes until the beef is browned, stirring frequently.

3 Add the beef stock and dark ale, cover and cook for 45–60 minutes, until the beef is almost cooked.

4 Add the milk, beans and salt and pepper and continue cooking until the beans and beef are tender. Add a little of the reserved bean liquid, if the stew begins to dry out. Adjust the seasoning and serve with steamed baby pattypan squash.

Caribbean Lamb Curry

This popular national dish of Jamaica is known as Curry Goat although goat meat or lamb can be used to make it.

INGREDIENTS

Serves 4–6
2 pounds boned leg of lamb
4 tablespoons curry powder
3 garlic cloves, crushed
1 large onion, chopped
4 thyme sprigs or 1 teaspoon dried thyme
3 bay leaves
1 teaspoon ground allspice
2 tablespoons vegetable oil
4 tablespoons butter or margarine
3¾ cups stock or water
1 fresh hot chili pepper, chopped
cooked rice, to serve
cilantro sprigs, to garnish

1 Cut the meat into 2-inch cubes, discarding any excess fat and gristle.

2 Place the lamb, curry powder, garlic, onion, thyme, bay leaves, allspice and oil in a large bowl and mix. Marinate in the fridge for at least 3 hours or overnight.

3 Melt the butter or margarine in a large heavy saucepan, add the seasoned lamb and fry over a moderate heat for about 10 minutes, turning the meat frequently.

4 Stir in the stock and chili pepper and bring to a boil. Reduce the heat, cover the pan and simmer for 1½ hours, or until the meat is tender. Serve with rice, garnish with cilantro.

COOK'S TIP

Try goat, or mutton, if you can and enjoy a robust curry.

Pork Roasted with Herbs, Spices and Rum

In the Caribbean, this spicy roast pork is usually barbecued and served on special occasions, as part of a buffet.

INGREDIENTS

Serves 6–8
2 garlic cloves, crushed
3 tablespoons soy sauce
1 tablespoon malt vinegar
1 tablespoon finely chopped celery
2 tablespoons chopped scallion
1½ teaspoons dried thyme
1 teaspoon dried sage
½ teaspoon allspice
2 teaspoons curry powder
½ cup rum
1 tablespoon raw sugar
3–3½-pound pork leg, boned and scored
salt and freshly ground black pepper
mashed sweet potato, to serve
scallion curls, to garnish

For the sauce
2 tablespoons butter or margarine
1 tablespoon tomato paste
1¼ cups stock
1 tablespoon chopped fresh parsley
1 tablespoon raw sugar
hot pepper sauce, to taste
salt

1 Mix together the garlic, soy sauce, vinegar, celery, scallions, thyme, sage, allspice, curry powder, rum, raw sugar and salt and pepper.

2 Open out the pork and slash the meat, without cutting through. Spread the mixture all over the pork, pressing it well into the slashes. Rub the outside of the leg with the mixture and refrigerate overnight.

3 Preheat the oven to 375°F. Roll the meat up, then tie tightly in several places with strong cotton string to hold the meat together.

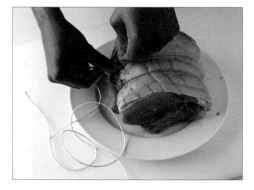

4 Spread a large piece of foil across a roasting pan and place the leg in the center. Baste the pork with a few spoonfuls of the marinade and wrap the foil around the leg, retaining the marinade.

5 Roast in the oven for 1¾ hours, then remove the foil, baste with any remaining marinade and cook for another hour. Check occasionally that the roast is not drying out and baste with any pan juices.

6 Transfer the pork to a warmed serving dish and leave to stand in a warm place for 15 minutes before serving. Meanwhile to start the sauce, pour the pan juices into a saucepan. Add the butter or margarine.

7 Add the tomato paste, stock, parsley, sugar, hot pepper and salt to taste. Simmer gently until reduced. Serve the pork sliced, with sweet potato. Garnish with scallion curls and pass the sauce separately.

COOK'S TIP

In the Caribbean pork is roasted until it is very well done, so reduce the cooking time to suit if you prefer meat slightly more juicy. To get the full flavor from the marinade, start to prepare the pork the night before you want to eat it.

Peppered Steak in Sherry Cream Sauce

This dish would be perfect for supper, served on a bed of noodles or with boiled plantains.

INGREDIENTS

Serves 4
1½ pounds steak
1 teaspoon spice seasoning
2 tablespoons butter
6–8 shallots, sliced
2 garlic cloves, crushed
½ cup sherry
3 tablespoons water
5 tablespoons light cream
salt and freshly ground black pepper
cooked plantain, to serve
chopped fresh chives, to garnish

1 Cut the meat into thin strips, discarding any fat or gristle.

2 Season the meat with pepper and spice seasoning and let marinate in a cool place for 30 minutes.

3 Melt the butter in a large frying pan and sauté the meat for 4–5 minutes until browned on all sides. Transfer to a plate and set aside.

4 Add the shallots and garlic to the pan, fry gently for a few minutes, then add the sherry and water and simmer for 5 minutes. Stir in the single cream.

5 Reduce the heat and adjust the seasoning. Stir in the meat and heat until hot but not boiling. Serve with plantain and garnish with chives.

Oxtail and Lima Beans

This is a traditional Caribbean stew; old-fashioned, economical, and good and spicy. It requires long cooking and lots of oxtail, but is a treat well worth the patience. As with many stews, it is delicious the next day, so make plenty.

INGREDIENTS

Serves 4 or more

3 pounds oxtail, chopped into pieces
7½ cups water
1 onion, finely chopped
3 bay leaves
4 thyme sprigs
3 whole cloves
6 ounces dried lima beans, soaked
  overnight
2 garlic cloves, crushed
1 tablespoon tomato paste
14-ounce can chopped tomatoes
1 teaspoon ground allspice
1 hot chili pepper
salt and freshly ground black pepper

1 Place the oxtail pieces in a large heavy pan, add the onion, bay leaves, thyme and cloves and cover with water. Bring to a boil, then reduce the heat.

2 Cover the pan and simmer for at least 2½ hours or until the meat is very tender, adding water whenever necessary.

3 Meanwhile, drain the beans and cover with water. Bring to a boil and simmer for 1–1¼ hours. Drain and set aside.

4 When the oxtail is cooked and the stock is well reduced, add the garlic, tomato paste, tomatoes, allspice, hot pepper, salt and black pepper. Add the lima beans and simmer for another 20 minutes. The stew should be fairly thick, but if it looks dry add a little water. Adjust the seasoning and serve.

Beef Pot Roast with Red Onions

The French-Caribbean culinary tradition of marinating and spicing meat has been used to create this mouth-warming spiced pot roast with an oriental touch. Use a heavy-based pan – a cast-iron casserole or Dutch oven is ideal – and simmer the beef over very low heat until it is meltingly tender.

Ingredients

Serves 6–8

3–4-pound boned and rolled top or
   bottom round roast of beef
1 tablespoon hoisin sauce
2 garlic cloves, crushed
1 tablespoon spice seasoning
1 red onion, thinly sliced
½ green pepper, thinly sliced
1¼ cups red wine
1¼ cups cold beef stock
fine cornmeal or all-purpose flour, for
   dusting
2 tablespoons vegetable oil
4 or 5 fresh basil leaves
basil sprigs, to garnish

1 Untie the rolled beef and open out on a flat surface. Spread with the hoisin sauce, garlic and half the spice seasoning and then sprinkle the onion, pepper and a few of the basil leaves on top. Fold over the end of the joint, roll up and re-tie with strong cotton string. Sprinkle with the remaining spice seasoning.

2 Place the meat in a large bowl and add enough wine and cold beef stock to cover. Cover the bowl loosely with plastic wrap and let the meat marinate in the fridge for several hours or overnight.

3 Remove the meat, reserving the marinade. Roll the roast in the cornmeal. Heat the oil in a large saucepan and brown the meat on all sides.

4 Lift the meat out onto a plate and drain off any excess oil. Return the meat to the pan and add the reserved marinade and basil.

5 Bring to a boil, then cover and simmer gently for about 2½ hours, or until the beef is tender.

6 Transfer the meat to a warmed serving plate and boil the cooking liquid until it is slightly syrupy and reduced by about half. Pour into a serving pitcher and serve with the meat, accompanied by mashed sweet potatoes and okra, and garnished with basil.

Variation

Shallots or Spanish onions can also be used. The beef can be roasted in the oven, rather than on top of the stove. Stock or water may be substituted for the wine.

"Seasoned-up" Lamb in Spinach Sauce

Lamb, spinach and ginger go well together. Powdered ginger has a strong distinctive flavor and should be used sparingly – you could use grated fresh ginger, if you prefer.

INGREDIENTS

Serves 4

1½ pounds stewing lamb, cubed
½ teaspoon ground ginger
½ teaspoon dried thyme
2 tablespoons olive oil
1 onion, chopped
2 garlic cloves, crushed
1 tablespoon tomato paste
½ hot chili pepper chopped (optional)
2½ cups stock or water
4 ounces fresh spinach, finely chopped
salt and freshly ground black pepper

1 Place the lamb in a glass or china dish, season with the ginger, thyme and salt and pepper and let marinate in a cool place for at least 2 hours or overnight in the fridge.

2 Heat the olive oil in a large heavy saucepan, add the onion and garlic and fry gently for 5 minutes or until the onion is soft.

3 Add the lamb, together with the tomato paste and hot pepper, if using. Fry over a moderate heat for about 5 minutes, stirring frequently, then add the stock or water. Cover and simmer for about 30 minutes, until the lamb is tender. Stir in the spinach. Simmer for 8 minutes until the sauce is fairly thick. Serve hot with boiled rice or root vegetables.

Lamb Pilaf

This dish was brought by East Indians to the West Indies.

INGREDIENTS

Serves 4

1 pound stewing lamb
1 tablespoon curry powder
1 onion, chopped
2 garlic cloves, crushed
½ teaspoon dried thyme
½ teaspoon dried oregano
1 fresh or dried chili
2 tablespoons butter or margarine, plus
   more for serving
2½ cups beef or chicken stock or
   coconut milk
1 teaspoon freshly ground black pepper
2 tomatoes, chopped
2 teaspoons sugar
2 tablespoons chopped scallions
1 pound basmati rice
scallion strips, to garnish

1 Cut the lamb into cubes and place in a shallow glass or china dish. Sprinkle with the curry powder, onion, garlic, herbs and chili and stir well. Cover loosely with plastic wrap and let marinate in a cool place for 1 hour.

2 Melt the butter or margarine in a saucepan and fry the lamb for 5–10 minutes on all sides. Add the stock or coconut milk, bring to a boil, then lower the heat and simmer for 35 minutes or until the meat is tender.

3 Add the black pepper, tomatoes, sugar, scallions and rice, stir well and reduce the heat. Make sure that the rice is covered by 1 inch of liquid and add a little water if necessary. Simmer the pilaf for 25 minutes or until the rice is cooked, then stir a little extra butter or margarine into the rice before serving. Garnish with scallion strips.

Barbecued Jerk Chicken

Jerk refers to the blend of herb and spice seasoning rubbed into meat, before it is roasted over charcoal sprinkled with pimiento berries. In Jamaica, jerk seasoning was originally used only for pork, but jerk chicken is equally good.

INGREDIENTS

Serves 4
8 chicken pieces

For the marinade
1 teaspoon ground allspice
1 teaspoon ground cinnamon
1 teaspoon dried thyme
¼ teaspoon freshly grated nutmeg
2 teaspoons raw sugar
2 garlic cloves, crushed
1 tablespoon finely chopped onion
1 tablespoon chopped scallion
1 tablespoon vinegar
2 tablespoons oil
1 tablespoon lime juice
1 hot chili pepper, chopped
salt and freshly ground black pepper
lettuce leaves, to serve

1 Combine all the marinade ingredients in a small bowl. Using a fork, mash them together well to make a thick paste.

2 Lay the chicken pieces on a plate or board and make several lengthwise slits in the flesh. Rub the seasoning all over the chicken and into the slits.

3 Place the chicken pieces in a dish, cover with plastic wrap and let marinate overnight in the fridge.

4 Shake off any excess seasoning from the chicken. Brush with oil and either place on a baking sheet or on a barbecue grill if barbecuing. Cook under a preheated broiler for 45 minutes, turning often. Or, if barbecuing, light the coals and when ready, cook over the coals for 30 minutes, turning often. Serve hot with lettuce leaves.

--- COOK'S TIP ---

The flavor is best if you marinate the chicken overnight. Sprinkle the charcoal with aromatic herbs such as bay leaves for even more flavor.

Thyme and Lime Chicken

INGREDIENTS

Serves 4

8 chicken thighs
2 tablespoons chopped scallion
1 teaspoon dried or chopped fresh thyme
2 garlic cloves, crushed
juice of 1 lime or lemon
6 tablespoons melted butter
salt and freshly ground black pepper
cooked rice, to serve
lime slices and cilantro sprigs,
    to garnish

1 Put the chicken thighs in an ovenproof dish or on a platter, skin-side down and, using a sharp knife, make a slit, lengthwise along the thigh bone of each thigh. Mix the scallion with a little salt and pepper and press the mixture into the slits.

2 Mix together the thyme, garlic, lime or lemon juice and all but 2 tablespoons of the butter in a small bowl and spoon over each chicken thigh.

3 Spoon the remaining butter over the top. Cover the chicken loosely with plastic wrap and let marinate in a cool place for several hours or overnight in the fridge.

4 Preheat the oven to 375°F. Remove the plastic wrap from the chicken and cover the dish with foil. Bake the chicken for 1 hour, then remove the foil and cook for a few more minutes to brown. Serve hot, with rice and garnish with lime slices and cilantro sprigs.

--- COOK'S TIP ---

You may need to use two limes, depending on their size and juiciness. Or, for a less sharp flavor, use lemons instead.

Spicy Fried Chicken

This crispy chicken is superb hot or cold. Served with a salad or vegetables, it makes a delicious lunch and is ideal for picnics or snacks too.

Ingredients

Serves 4–6
4 chicken drumsticks
4 chicken thighs
2 teaspoons curry powder
½ teaspoon garlic powder
½ teaspoon ground black pepper
½ teaspoon paprika
1¼ cups milk
oil, for deep frying
4 tablespoons all-purpose flour
salt
lettuce leaves, to serve

1 Place the chicken pieces in a large bowl and sprinkle with the curry powder, garlic powder, black pepper, paprika and salt. Rub the spices well into the chicken, then cover and let marinate in a cool place for at least 2 hours, or overnight in the fridge.

2 Preheat the oven to 350°F. Pour enough milk into the bowl to cover the chicken and leave to stand for a further 15 minutes.

3 Heat the oil in a large saucepan or deep-fat fryer and sprinkle the flour onto a plate. Shake off excess milk, dip each piece of chicken in flour and fry two or three pieces at a time until golden, but not cooked. Continue until all the chicken pieces are fried.

4 Remove with a slotted spoon, place the chicken pieces on a baking sheet, and bake for about 30 minutes. Serve hot or cold with lettuce leaves.

Sunday Roast Chicken

INGREDIENTS

Serves 6

3–3½-pound chicken
1 teaspoon paprika
1 teaspoon dried thyme
½ teaspoon dried tarragon
1 teaspoon garlic powder
1 tablespoon lemon juice
2 tablespoons honey
3 tablespoons dark rum
melted butter, for basting
1¼ cups chicken stock
lime quarters, to garnish

1 Place the chicken in a roasting tin and mix the paprika, thyme, tarragon, garlic powder and salt and pepper together. Rub all over the chicken, lifting the skin and spreading the seasoning underneath it too. Cover the chicken loosely with plastic wrap and let marinate in a cool place for at least 2 hours or preferably overnight in the fridge.

2 Preheat the oven to 375°F. Blend together the lemon juice, honey and rum and pour over and under the skin of the chicken, rubbing it in well.

COOK'S TIP

Extra herbs and rum can be used to make a richer, very tasty gravy, if you like.

3 Spoon the melted butter all over the chicken, then transfer to the oven and roast for 1½–2 hours.

4 Pour the pan juices from the chicken into a small saucepan. Keep the chicken warm while you make the sauce. Add the chicken stock to the pan and simmer over a low heat for 10 minutes or until reduced. Adjust the seasoning and pour into a serving pitcher. Serve with the chicken and garnish with lime quarters.

Peanut Chicken

Natural peanut butter makes a rich nutty sauce, but you can make your own using peanuts crushed in a food processor, with excellent results.

INGREDIENTS

Serves 4

2 chicken breasts, boned and skinned and cut into pieces.
2 garlic cloves, crushed
½ teaspoon dried thyme
½ teaspoon freshly ground black pepper
1 tablespoon curry powder
1 tablespoon lemon juice
2 tablespoons butter or margarine
1 onion, chopped
3 tablespoons chopped tomatoes
1 hot chili pepper, chopped
2 tablespoons smooth peanut butter
salt
fried plantain, to serve
cilantro sprigs, to garnish

1 Place the chicken pieces into a large bowl and stir in the garlic, thyme, black pepper, curry powder, lemon juice and a little salt. Cover loosely with plastic wrap and let marinate in a cool place for a few hours.

2 Melt the butter or margarine in a large saucepan, add the onion and sauté gently for 5 minutes, then add the seasoned chicken. Fry over a medium heat for 10 minutes, turning frequently, and then add the tomatoes and the hot pepper and stir well.

3 Blend the peanut butter with a little warm water to a smooth paste and stir into the chicken mixture.

4 Slowly stir in 1¾ cups warm water and simmer gently for about 30 minutes, adding a little more water if necessary. Serve the chicken hot with fried plantain and garnished with cilantro sprigs.

Breast of Turkey with Mango and Wine

Fresh mango gives this dish a truly tropical taste.

INGREDIENTS

Serves 4

4 turkey breast fillets
1 garlic clove, crushed
¼ teaspoon ground cinnamon
1 tablespoon finely chopped fresh parsley
1 tablespoon crushed pilot crackers
2 tablespoons chopped ripe mango
3 tablespoons butter or margarine, softened
1 garlic clove, crushed
6 shallots, sliced
⅔ cup white wine
salt and freshly ground black pepper
diced fresh mango and chopped fresh parsley, to garnish

1 Cut a slit horizontally through each turkey breast to make a "pocket".

2 Put the crushed garlic, cinnamon, parsley, cracker crumbs, mango, 1 tablespoon of the butter or margarine and salt and pepper in a bowl and mash together. Spoon a little mixture into each of the "pockets" and if necessary secure with a wooden toothpick. Season with a little extra pepper.

3 Melt the remaining butter or margarine in a large frying pan and sauté the garlic and shallots for 5 minutes. Add the turkey and cook for 15 minutes, turning once. Add the wine, cover and simmer gently, until the turkey is fully cooked. Add the diced mango, heat through for a minute or two and serve, garnished with the parsley.

BREADS AND SIDE DISHES

Meat and fish dishes are never served alone in the Caribbean, but are always accompanied by side dishes. Almost all filling or carbohydrate-rich foods like rice, beans, potatoes and bread are popular in the Caribbean, although rice, whether simply boiled, or cooked with peas or vegetables is most widely eaten. Peas and Rice is a traditional dish throughout the Caribbean, although variations do occur, such as in the eastern Caribbean islands and Guyana, where pigeon peas take the place of red kidney beans. Some side dishes such as Eggplant with Garlic and Scallions are excellent by themselves, and can be served as a main meal with Rice and Peas, and salad.

Dhal Puri

Otherwise known as roti, these thin fried breads can also be made with white flour. They are delicious served with meat, fish or vegetable dishes.

INGREDIENTS

Makes about 15

4 cups self-rising flour
1 cup whole wheat flour
1½ cups cold water
2 tablespoons oil, plus extra for frying
salt, to taste

For the filling

12 ounces yellow split peas
1 tablespoon ground cumin
2 garlic cloves, crushed

1 Sift together the dry ingredients into a bowl, then add the water a little at a time gradually kneading the mixture to make a soft dough. Knead for a short while until supple.

2 Add the oil to the dough and continue to knead until completely smooth. Put the dough in a plastic bag or wrap in plastic wrap and let stand in a cool place or in the fridge for at least 30 minutes, or overnight.

3 To make the filling, put the peas in a saucepan, cover with water and cook until the peas are half cooked – they should be tender on the outside, but still firm in the middle. Allow the water to evaporate during cooking, until the pan is dry, but watch carefully and add a little extra water to prevent burning, if necessary.

4 Spread the peas out onto a tray to cool, then grind to a paste and mix with the cumin and garlic.

5 Divide the dough into about 15 balls. Slightly flatten each ball of dough, put about 1 tablespoon of mixture into the center and fold over the edges to enclose the mixture.

6 Dust a rolling pin and a board with flour and roll out the dhal puri, taking care not to overstretch, until they are about 7 inches in diameter.

7 Heat a little oil on a tawa (roti pan) or in a heavy or cast-iron frying pan, swirling the oil to cover the base. Cook the dhal puris for about 3 minutes on each side, until light brown. Fold them into a clean dish towel, to keep warm. Serve warm.

Fried Dumplings

Fried Dumplings or "dumplins" are easy to make and the "sister" to Bakes, as they are also known in the Caribbean and Guyana. They are usually served with salt cod or fried fish, but they can be eaten quite simply with butter and jam or cheese. Children love them!

INGREDIENTS

Makes about 10
4 cups self-rising flour
2 teaspoons sugar
½ teaspoon salt
1¼ cups milk
oil, for frying

1 Sift the dry ingredients together into a large bowl, add the milk and mix and knead until smooth.

2 Divide the dough into ten balls, kneading each ball with floured hands. Press the balls gently to flatten into 3-inch rounds.

3 Heat a little oil in a nonstick frying pan until moderately hot. Place half the dumplings in the pan, reduce the heat to low and fry for about 15 minutes until they are golden brown, turning once.

4 Stand them on their sides for a few minutes to brown the edges, before removing them and draining on paper towels. Serve warm.

Pigeon Peas Cook-Up Rice

This Guyanese-style rice dish is made with the most commonly used peas.

INGREDIENTS

Serves 4–6
2 tablespoons butter or margarine
1 medium onion, chopped
1 garlic clove, crushed
2 tablespoons chopped scallion
1 large carrot, diced
1 cup pigeon peas
1 thyme sprig or 1 teaspoon dried thyme
1 cinnamon stick
2½ cups vegetable stock
4 tablespoons coconut cream
1 hot chili pepper, chopped
2¼ cups long grain rice
salt and freshly ground black pepper

1 Melt the butter or margarine in a large heavy saucepan, add the onion and garlic and sauté over a medium heat for 5 minutes, stirring occasionally.

2 Add the scallion, carrot, pigeon peas, thyme, cinnamon, stock, coconut cream, hot pepper and seasoning and bring to a boil.

3 Reduce the heat and then stir in the rice. Cover and simmer gently over a low heat until all the liquid is absorbed and the rice is tender.

4 Stir with a fork to fluff up the rice before serving.

--- COOK'S TIP ---

Pigeon peas are also known as gunga peas. The fresh peas can be difficult to obtain, but you will find them in specialty shops. The frozen peas are green and the canned variety are brown. Drain the salted water from canned peas and rinse before using them in this recipe.

Green Bananas and Yam in Coconut Milk

INGREDIENTS

Serves 3–4
4 green bananas, peeled and halved
1 pound white yam, peeled and cut into pieces
1 thyme sprig
1½ ounces coconut cream
salt and freshly ground black pepper
chopped fresh thyme, and thyme sprigs, to garnish

1 Bring 3¾ cups water to a boil in a large saucepan, reduce the heat and add the green bananas and yam. Simmer gently for about 10 minutes.

2 Add the thyme, coconut and seasoning, bring back to a boil and cook over a moderate heat until the yam and banana are tender.

3 Transfer the yam and banana to a plate with a slotted spoon and continue cooking the coconut milk until thick and creamy.

4 When the sauce is ready, return vegetables to the pan and heat through. Spoon into a warmed serving dish, sprinkle with chopped thyme and garnish with thyme sprigs.

Cou-Cou

A specialty of Barbados, this goes well with flying fish but can be served with any other fish, meat or vegetable stew.

INGREDIENTS

Serves 4
4 ounces okra, ends removed and sliced
8 ounces coarse cornmeal
2½ cups water or coconut milk
2 tablespoons butter, softened
salt and freshly ground black pepper

1 Cook the okra in boiling water seasoned with a little salt and pepper for about 10 minutes. Drain and reserve the cooking liquid.

2 Bring half of the reserved liquid to a boil in a separate pan, add the okra and then beat in the cornmeal.

3 Cook over a very low heat, beating the mixture vigorously. Add the water or coconut milk, a little at a time, beating after each addition, to keep it from sticking to the bottom of the pan and burning.

4 Cover and continue to cook over low heat for about 20 minutes, beating occasionally. When the cornmeal granules are soft the cou-cou is cooked. Turn off heat, cover with foil and then a lid to keep moist and hot, until ready to serve. Spread the top with butter before serving.

Rice and Peas

This very popular dish also known as Peas and Rice on the islands in the Eastern Caribbean is far more interesting and tasty than its name suggests.

INGREDIENTS

Serves 6

6 ounces red kidney beans
2 fresh thyme sprigs
¼ cup coconut cream
2 bay leaves
1 onion, finely chopped
2 garlic cloves, crushed
½ teaspoon ground allspice
4 ounces chopped, red or green bell
  pepper
2 cups long grain rice
salt and freshly ground black pepper

1 Place the red kidney beans in a large bowl. Cover with water and let soak overnight.

2 Drain the beans, place in a large pan and add enough water to cover the beans by about 1 inch. Bring to a boil and boil over a high heat for 10 minutes, then reduce the heat and simmer for about 1½ hours or until the beans are tender.

3 Add the thyme, coconut cream, bay leaves, onion, garlic, allspice, red or green bell pepper and seasoning and stir in 2½ cups water.

4 Bring to a boil and add the rice. Stir well, reduce the heat and simmer, covered, for 25–30 minutes, until all the liquid is absorbed. Serve as an accompaniment to fish, meat or vegetarian dishes.

Buttered Spinach and Rice

The spinach, usually mixed in with the rice but once forgotten, was then added as a topping and became a favorite.

INGREDIENTS

Serves 4
3 tablespoons butter or margarine
1 onion, finely chopped
2 fresh tomatoes, chopped
1 pound basmati rice, washed
2 garlic cloves, crushed
2½ cups stock or water
12 ounces fresh spinach, shredded
salt and freshly ground black pepper
2 tomatoes, sliced, to garnish

1 Melt 2 tablespoons of the butter or margarine in a large heavy saucepan and fry the onion for a few minutes until soft. Add the chopped tomatoes and stir well.

2 Add the rice and garlic, cook for 5 minutes, then gradually add the stock, stirring all the time. Season well.

3 Cover and simmer gently for 10–15 minutes or until the rice is almost cooked, then reduce the heat to low.

4 Spread the spinach in a thick layer over the rice. Cover the pan and cook over a low heat for 5–8 minutes until the spinach has wilted. Dot the remaining butter over the top and then serve, garnished with sliced tomatoes.

COOK'S TIP

If fresh spinach is not available, you can use frozen leaf spinach instead. Thaw and drain 8 ounces frozen spinach and cook as in the recipe for about 3–5 minutes. Finely shredded collard greens can also be used.

Mashed Sweet Potatoes

White sweet potatoes are best for this recipe, rather than orange sweet potatoes. White yams make a good substitute, especially poona (Ghanaian) yam.

INGREDIENTS

Serves 4
2 pounds sweet potatoes
4 tablespoons butter
3 tablespoons light cream
freshly grated nutmeg
1 tablespoon chopped fresh chives
salt and freshly ground black pepper

1 Peel the sweet potatoes under cold running water and place in a bowl of salted water. Cut or slice them and place in a large saucepan and cover with cold water. Cook, covered for about 30 minutes.

2 When the potatoes are cooked, drain and add the butter, cream, nutmeg, chives and seasoning. Mash with a potato masher and then fluff up with a fork. Serve warm as an accompaniment to a curry or stew.

Corn Sticks

This recipe produces perfect corn bread in a loaf tin, or makes attractive corn sticks, if you can find the molds.

INGREDIENTS

Makes 40 corn sticks
2 cups all-purpose flour
1½ cups fine cornmeal
10 teaspoons baking powder
½ teaspoon salt
4 tablespoons demerara sugar
1⅞ cups milk
2 eggs
4 tablespoons butter or margarine

1 Preheat the oven to 375°F and grease either corn bread molds or a 2-pound loaf pan.

2 Sift together the flour, cornmeal, baking powder, salt and sugar into a large bowl. In a separate bowl, whisk the milk and eggs, then stir into the flour mixture.

3 Melt the butter or margarine in a small pan and stir into the mixture.

4 Spoon the mixture into the molds or tin. Bake the corn sticks for 15 minutes. If using a loaf pan, bake for 30–35 minutes, until golden and hollow sounding when tapped.

COOK'S TIP

Because there is such a lot of baking powder, the cornmeal mixture begins to rise as soon as liquid is added, so bake the corn sticks or bread right away.

Fried Yellow Plantains

When plantains are yellow, they are ripe and ready to enhance most meat, fish or vegetarian dishes. The riper the plantain, the darker and sweeter they are.

INGREDIENTS

Serves 4
2 yellow plantains
oil, for shallow frying
finely chopped chives, to garnish

1 Using a small sharp knife, remove the ends of the plantains, and cut in half.

2 Slit the skin only, along the natural ridges of each plantain.

3 Ease up the edge of the skin and run the tip of your thumb along the plantains, lifting the skin.

4 Peel away the skin and slice the plantains lengthwise. Heat a little oil in a large frying pan and fry the plantain slices for 2–3 minutes on each side until golden brown.

5 When brown and crisp, drain on paper towels and serve hot or cold, sprinkled with chives.

Okra Fried Rice

INGREDIENTS

Serves 3–4

2 tablespoons vegetable oil
1 tablespoon butter or margarine
1 garlic clove, crushed
½ red onion, finely chopped
4 ounces okra, ends removed
2 tablespoons diced green and red bell
  pepper
½ teaspoon dried thyme
2 green chilies, finely chopped
½ teaspoon five-spice powder
1 vegetable stock cube
2 tablespoons soy sauce
1 tablespoon chopped cilantro
1¼ cups cooked rice
salt and freshly ground black pepper
cilantro sprigs, to garnish

1 Heat the oil and butter or margarine in a frying pan or wok, add the garlic and onion and cook over a moderate heat for 5 minutes until soft.

2 Thinly slice the okra, add to the pan or wok and sauté gently for 6–7 minutes.

3 Add the green and red peppers, thyme, chilies and five-spice powder and cook for 3 minutes.

4 Add the stock cube, soy sauce, cilantro and rice and heat through, stirring well to mix. Season to taste with salt and pepper. Serve hot, garnished with cilantro sprigs.

Eggplant with Garlic and Scallions

This is my favorite way of serving eggplant – you can make it even more delicious by adding smoked salmon.

INGREDIENTS

Serves 4

3 tablespoons vegetable oil
2 garlic cloves, crushed
3 tomatoes, peeled and chopped
2 pounds eggplant, chopped
⅔ cup vegetable stock or water
2 tablespoons soy sauce
4 tablespoons chopped scallions
½ red bell pepper, chopped
1 hot chili pepper, chopped
1 tablespoon chopped fresh cilantro
salt and freshly ground black pepper

1 Heat the oil in a wok or large frying pan and fry the garlic and tomatoes for a few minutes until slightly softened. Add the eggplants and toss together with the garlic and tomatoes.

2 Add the stock or water and cover the pan. Simmer gently until the eggplants are very soft.

3 Add the soy sauce, half of the scallions, red pepper, hot pepper and seasoning and stir well.

4 Sprinkle with the remaining chopped scallions and serve.

CAKES, DESSERTS AND DRINKS

Tropical fruits and nuts flavored with spices are the basis of many of the recipes in this section. In the Caribbean, people eat fresh fruits and nuts "au naturel" at any time of day. However, both fresh and dried fruits are also used widely in desserts, cakes, and homemade breads as well as in a variety of superb fruit drinks, alcoholic cocktails and punches. Nowadays, almost all popular Caribbean fruits can be found throughout the year in most large supermarkets and West Indian delicatessens. If fresh fruit is not available, then use canned fruit instead.

Caribbean Fruit and Rum Cake

My mother's recipe for a cake that is eaten at Christmas, weddings and other special occasions. It is known as Black Cake, because, traditionally, the recipe usually uses burned sugar.

INGREDIENTS

Makes one 10-inch round cake

2 cups currants
3 cups raisins
1 cup prunes, pitted
⅔ cup mixed citrus peel
2¼ cups dark brown sugar
1 teaspoon ground cinnamon
6 tablespoons rum, plus more if needed
1¼ cups sherry, plus more if needed
1 pound/2 cups softened butter
10 eggs, beaten
1 pound/4 cups self-rising flour
1 teaspoon vanilla extract

1 Wash the currants, raisins, prunes and mixed peel, then pat dry. Place in a food processor and process until finely chopped. Transfer to a large, clean jar or bowl, add ¾ cup of the sugar, the mixed spice, rum and sherry. Mix very well and then cover with a lid and set aside for anything from 2 weeks to 3 months – the longer it is left, the better the flavor will be.

2 Stir the fruit mixture occasionally and keep covered, adding more rum and sherry, if you like.

3 Preheat the oven to 325°F. Grease and line a 10-inch round cake pan with a double layer of wax paper.

4 Sift the flour, and set aside. Cream together the butter and remaining sugar and beat in the eggs until the mixture is smooth and creamy.

5 Add the fruit mixture, then gradually stir in the flour and vanilla extract. Mix well, adding 1–2 tablespoons sherry if the mixture is too stiff; it should just fall off the back of the spoon, but should not be too runny.

6 Spoon the mixture into the prepared pan, cover loosely with foil and bake for about 2½ hours until the cake is firm and springy. Leave to cool in the pan overnight, then sprinkle with more rum if the cake is not to be used immediately. Wrap the cake in foil to keep it moist.

--- COOK'S TIP ---

Although the dried fruits are chopped in a food processor, they can be marinated whole, if preferred. If you don't have enough time to marinate the fruit, simmer the fruit in the liquor mixture for about 30 minutes, and leave overnight.

Barbadian Coconut Sweet Bread

Often made at Christmas time, this delicious coconut bread is most enjoyable with a cup of hot chocolate or a glass of fruit punch.

INGREDIENTS

Makes 1 large or two small loaves

¾ cup butter or margarine
⅔ cup raw sugar
2 cups self-rising flour
scant 2 cups all-purpose flour
4 ounces dried coconut
1 teaspoon ground cinnamon
2 teaspoons vanilla extract
1 tablespoon rum (optional)
2 eggs
⅔ cup milk
1 tablespoon superfine sugar, blended with 2 tablespoons water, to glaze

1 Preheat the oven to 350°F. Grease two 1-pound loaf pans or one 2-pound pan.

2 Place the butter or margarine and sugar in a large bowl and sift in the flour. Rub the ingredients together with your fingertips until the mixture resembles fine bread crumbs.

3 Add the coconut, mixed spice, vanilla extract, rum if using, eggs and milk and mix together well with your hands. If the mixture is too dry, moisten with milk. Knead on a floured board until firm and pliable.

4 Halve the mixture and place in the prepared loaf pans. Glaze with sugared water and bake for about 1 hour or until the loaves are cooked. The loaves are ready when a skewer pushed into the center comes out clean.

Duckanoo

This tasty pudding originated in west Africa.

INGREDIENTS

Serves 4–6

1 pound/3 cups fine cornmeal
12 ounces fresh coconut, chopped
2½ cups fresh milk
¾ cup raisins
4 tablespoons butter or margarine, melted
½ cup raw sugar
4 tablespoons water
¼ teaspoon freshly grated nutmeg
½ teaspoon ground cinnamon
1 teaspoon vanilla extract

1 Place the cornmeal in a large bowl. Blend the coconut and the milk in a blender or food processor until smooth. Stir the coconut mixture into the cornmeal, then add all the remaining ingredients and stir well.

2 Take six pieces of foil and fold into 5- x 6-inch pockets leaving an opening on one short side. Fold the edges of the remaining sides tightly to make sure that they are well sealed.

3 Put one or two spoonfuls of the mixture into each pocket and fold over the edge of the foil to seal.

4 Place the foil pockets in a large saucepan of boiling water. Cover and simmer for about 45–60 minutes. Lift out the pockets from the water and remove the foil. Serve the duckanoo by themselves or with fresh cream.

Apple and Cinnamon Crumble Cake

This fantastic cake has layers of spicy fruit and crumble and is quite delicious served warm with fresh cream.

INGREDIENTS

Makes 1 cake
3 large cooking apples
½ teaspoon ground cinnamon
1 cup butter
1¼ cups superfine sugar
4 eggs
4 cups self-rising flour

For the crumble topping
¾ cup raw sugar
1¼ cups all-purpose flour
1 teaspoon ground cinnamon
about 4½ tablespoons dried coconut
½ cup butter

1 Preheat the oven to 350°F. Grease a 10-inch round cake pan and line the base with wax paper. To make the crumble topping, mix together the sugar, flour, cinnamon and coconut in a bowl, then rub in the butter with your fingertips and set aside.

2 Peel and core the apples, then grate them coarsely. Place them in a bowl, sprinkle with the cinnamon and set aside.

3 Cream the butter and sugar in a bowl with an electric mixer, until light and fluffy. Beat in the eggs, one at a time, beating well after each addition.

4 Sift in half the flour, mix well, then add the remaining flour and stir until smooth.

5 Spread half the cake mixture evenly over the bottom of the prepared pan. Spoon the apples on top and sprinkle over half the crumble topping.

6 Spread the remaining cake mixture over the crumble and finally top with the remaining crumble topping.

7 Bake for 1 hour 10 minutes – 1 hour 20 minutes, covering the cake with foil if it browns too quickly. Leave in the pan for about 5 minutes before turning out onto a wire rack. Once cool, cut into slices to serve.

COOK'S TIP

To make the topping in a food processor, add all the ingredients and process for a few seconds until the mixture resembles bread crumbs. You can also grate the apples using the grating disk. If you don't have a 10-inch round pan you can use a 8-inch square cake pan.

Bread and Butter Custard

This dessert is a delicious family favorite. A richer version can be made with fresh cream instead of evaporated milk. It can also be made using other dried fruit – mango is particularly good.

INGREDIENTS

Serves 4

1 tablespoon softened butter
3 thin slices of bread, crusts removed
14-ounce can evaporated milk
⅔ cup fresh milk
½ teaspoon ground cinnamon
3 tablespoons raw sugar
2 eggs, whisked
½ cup golden raisins
freshly grated nutmeg
a little confectioner's sugar, for dusting

1 Preheat the oven to 350°F and lightly butter an ovenproof dish. Butter the bread and cut into small pieces.

2 Lay the buttered bread in several layers in the prepared dish.

3 Whisk together the evaporated milk and the fresh milk, mixed spice, sugar and eggs in a large bowl. Pour the mixture over the bread and butter. Sprinkle over the raisins and let stand for 30 minutes.

4 Grate a little nutmeg over the top and bake for 30–40 minutes until the custard is just set and golden. Serve sprinkled with confectioner's sugar.

Avocado Salad in Ginger and Orange Sauce

This is an unusual fruit salad since avocado is more often treated as a vegetable. However, in the Caribbean it is used as a fruit, which of course it is!

INGREDIENTS

Serves 4
2 firm ripe avocados
3 firm ripe bananas, chopped
12 fresh cherries or strawberries
juice of 1 large orange
shredded fresh ginger root (optional)

For the ginger syrup
2 ounces fresh ginger root, chopped
3³/₄ cups water
1 cup raw sugar
2 cloves

1 First make the ginger syrup; place the ginger, water, sugar and cloves in a saucepan and bring to a boil. Reduce the heat and simmer for about 1 hour, until well reduced and syrupy.

2 Remove the ginger and discard and set aside to cool. Store in a covered container in the fridge.

3 Peel the avocados, cut into cubes and place in a bowl with the bananas and cherries or strawberries.

4 Pour the orange juice over the fruits. Add 4 tablespoons of the ginger syrup and mix gently, using a metal spoon. Chill for 30 minutes and add a little shredded ginger, if using.

Fruits of the Tropics Salad

INGREDIENTS

Serves 4–6

1 medium pineapple
14-ounce can guava halves in syrup
2 medium bananas, sliced
1 large mango, peeled, pitted and diced
4 ounces preserved ginger and
  2 tablespoons of the syrup
4 tablespoons thick coconut milk
2 teaspoons sugar
½ teaspoon freshly grated nutmeg
½ teaspoon ground cinnamon
strips of coconut, to decorate

1 Peel, core and cube the pineapple, and place in a serving bowl. Drain the guavas, reserve the syrup and chop. Add the guavas to the bowl with one of the bananas and the mango.

2 Chop the preserved ginger and add to the pineapple mixture.

3 Pour 2 tablespoons of the ginger syrup, and the reserved guava syrup into a blender or food processor and add the other banana, the coconut milk and the sugar. Blend to make a smooth creamy purée.

4 Pour the banana and coconut mixture over the fruit, add a little grated nutmeg and a sprinkling of cinnamon. Serve chilled, decorated with strips of coconut.

Coconut Ice Cream

An easy-to-make heavenly ice cream that will be loved by all for its tropical taste. Lemon balm, an easily grown herb, gives it a spicy fragrance.

INGREDIENTS

Serves 8
14-ounce can evaporated milk
14-ounce can condensed milk
14-ounce can coconut milk
freshly grated nutmeg
1 teaspoon almond extract
lemon balm sprigs, lime slices and
    shredded coconut, to decorate

1 Mix together the evaporated, condensed and coconut milks in a large freezerproof bowl and stir in the nutmeg and almond extract.

2 Chill in a freezer for an hour or two until the mixture is semi-frozen.

3 Remove from the freezer and whisk the mixture with a hand or electric whisk until it is fluffy and almost doubled in volume.

4 Pour into a freezer container, then cover and freeze. Soften slightly before serving, decorated with lemon balm, lime slices and shredded coconut.

Spiced Pineapple Punch

INGREDIENTS

Serves 3–4
6¼ cups pineapple juice
14-ounce can condensed milk
1 teaspoon vanilla extract
freshly grated nutmeg
pinch of ground cinnamon
lime juice, to serve

> ──── COOK'S TIP ────
>
> If you don't have a blender or food processor,
> just pour the pineapple juice and milk into a
> large bowl and whisk vigorously to mix.

1 Pour the pineapple juice into a blender or food processor. Add all of the condensed milk and the vanilla extract and process for a few seconds, until the juice and milk are well blended.

2 Add the grated nutmeg and cinnamon and blend for a few more seconds. Chill the punch until very cold and serve with ice and a squeeze of lime.

Sarah's Island Mist Fruit Punch

Memories of sipping fruit punch and feasting on mangoes in the St Lucian hills on beautiful misty mornings provided the inspiration for this delicious summery drink.

INGREDIENTS

2 bananas
4 tablespoons ginger syrup
½ teaspoon almond essence
½ teaspoon vanilla essence
4 cups mango juice
3⅔ cups pineapple juice
1 cup lemonade
freshly grated nutmeg
lemon balm and orange slices,
    to decorate

> ──── COOK'S TIP ────
>
> Prepare this punch up to 2 hours in
> advance and chill until ready to serve.

1 Peel the bananas and chop them into ½-inch pieces.

2 Blend the bananas, ginger syrup and essences in a blender or food processor until smooth.

3 Pour the mixture to a large punch bowl. Stir in the mango and pineapple juices, then pour in the lemonade. Finish by sprinkling in some grated nutmeg. Serve chilled, decorated with lemon balm and orange slices.

Demerara Rum Punch

The inspiration for this punch
came from the rum distillery at
Plantation Diamond Estate in
Guyana where some of the finest
rum in the world is made, and
the tantalizing aromas of sugar
cane and rum pervade the air.

INGREDIENTS

Serves 4
²⁄₃ cup orange juice
²⁄₃ cup pineapple juice
²⁄₃ cup mango juice
½ cup water
1 cup dark rum
a shake of Angostura bitters
freshly grated nutmeg
2 tablespoons raw sugar
1 small banana
1 large orange

1 Pour the orange, pineapple and
mango juices into a large punch
bowl. Stir in the water.

2 Add the rum, Angostura bitters,
nutmeg and sugar. Stir gently for a
few minutes until the sugar has dissolved.

3 Slice the banana and stir gently into
the punch.

4 Slice the orange and add to the
punch. Chill and serve with ice.

COOK'S TIP

You can use white rum instead of dark, if
you prefer. To make a stronger punch, add
more rum.

Caribbean Cream Stout Punch

A well-known "pick-me-up" that is popular all over the Caribbean.

INGREDIENTS

Serves 2

2 cups stout
1¼ cups evaporated milk
5 tablespoons condensed milk
5 tablespoons sherry
2 or 3 drops vanilla extract
freshly grated nutmeg

1 Mix together the stout, evaporated and condensed milks, sherry and vanilla extract in a blender or food processor, or whisk together in a large mixing bowl, until creamy.

2 Add a little grated nutmeg to the stout mixture and blend or whisk again for a few minutes.

3 Chill for at least 45 minutes or until really cold before serving.

Index